# YOUR KNOWLEDGE HAS VALUE

Richards Macdonald

# Unilever. A Strategic Analysis

GRIN Verlag

**Bibliografische Information der Deutschen Nationalbibliothek:**

Die Deutsche Bibliothek verzeichnet diese Publikation in der Deutschen National-bibliografie; detaillierte bibliografische Daten sind im Internet über http://dnb.d-nb.de/ abrufbar.

**Imprint:**

Copyright © 2012 GRIN Verlag GmbH
Druck und Bindung: Books on Demand GmbH, Norderstedt Germany
ISBN: 978-3-656-45835-7

**This book at GRIN:**

http://www.grin.com/en/e-book/215742/unilever-a-strategic-analysis

**GRIN - Your knowledge has value**

Der GRIN Verlag publiziert seit 1998 wissenschaftliche Arbeiten von Studenten, Hochschullehrern und anderen Akademikern als eBook und gedrucktes Buch. Die Verlagswebsite www.grin.com ist die ideale Plattform zur Veröffentlichung von Hausarbeiten, Abschlussarbeiten, wissenschaftlichen Aufsätzen, Dissertationen und Fachbüchern.

**Visit us on the internet:**

http://www.grin.com/

http://www.facebook.com/grincom

http://www.twitter.com/grin_com

**Executive Summary**

Unilever is a London-based fast-moving consumer goods company that sells its products in nearly 200 countries. However, it is neither the largest packaged consumer goods or food company as it has fiercely competitive rivals. In recent years, new corporate leadership has instituted changes, including a new mission and a new vision. These have resulted in a more positive relationship with consumers, a better public image, and an increasing presence in developing countries. Still, our strategic analysis of the company shows impending threats that can damage Unilever's margin of profit and global stake in the fast-moving consumer goods industry. New brands, mounting competition, and an increase in taxation and regulations are mounting obstacles to Unilever's continued success. In order to overcome these and other future vulnerabilities, Unilever needs to continue its product and information technologies developments, introspection, campaigns, and external monitoring.

**Company Profile**

Unilever is an Anglo-Dutch company that consists of over 400 brands "focused on health and wellbeing" (Unilever, 2013a). Unilever sells its products to more than 190 countries and belongs to the fast-moving consumer goods (FMCG) industry. Specifically, it is the second largest packaged consumer goods firm after Proctor & Gamble (P&G), and it is the third largest food company after Nestle and Kraft Foods. While Unilever is based in London, England, it sells food, home, and personal care products over all major continents. Unilever was formed when the Dutch margarine company Margarine Unie merged with the British soapmaker Lever Brothers in 1930. The two companies decide to combine since they were often competing for the same raw materials, oils and fats, to make their products. Today, Unilever has adopted a new mission to focus on twenty-first century consumers alongside its new corporate vision to "create a better future every day" (Unilever, 2013b).

**Strategic Analysis**

Strategic analysis is an examination of a company in order to determine its future direction or to better understand the best prospective pursuits (Armstrong, 1986). In order to realize Unilever's current and future strategies, we have undertaken three different methods of strategic analysis – PESTEL, Porter's Five Forces, and SWOT. In order to give a thorough analysis of Unilever, we will use these three methods to identify the industrial, internal, and

external factors that impact the company's future.

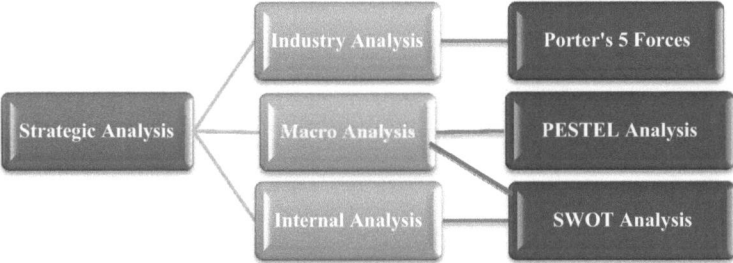

**PESTEL Analysis**

PESTEL analysis focuses on the external environment in which a company exists. This form of macro-analysis consists of an inquiry into a firm's political, economic, social, technological, environmental, and legal environment. The goal of this analysis is to align the company's vision and performance with the business environment.

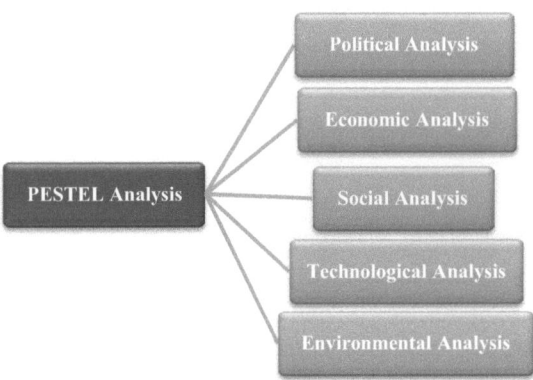

*Political & Legal Analysis*

Due to Unilever's widespread commerce, it is subject to laws, regulations, and politics of every country, region, and locality is sells its products in. Consequently, Unilever has developed a tactical response to political and legal issues. Unilever must continue to adhere to regulations in every country in which they distribute their products. Furthermore, it must adhere to emerging regulations such as new low-impact environmental policies. Changing free trade policies, especially within the European Union, can have adverse effects on potential profits. Ultimately, any political or legal strife would damage Unilever's

reputation in the marketplace and therefore the company's profits (Unilever Communications, 2013).

*Economic Analysis*

The current world economic climate has taken a toll on large corporations at the same time that the consumer goods market is highly competitive. All events that currently threaten large countries' economies also affect Unilever. Consequently, the current worldwide recession has the potential to hurt Unilever's profits. Governments' responses to this fiscal crisis, such as stimulus plans, changes in taxation, and price controls can majorly affect Unilever. In particular, the increase in British taxes, inflation of food prices, rising oil costs, fluctuations in currencies, and income disparity all have the potential to take a large toll on the FMCG company (Steiner, 2010; World Economic Forum, 2013). Furthermore, industry competition, portfolio management, and business transformation also pose risks to Unilever.

*Social Analysis*

Unilever serves as a good model for a company that is trying to positively impact on global sociological and health problems, or as they term "acting responsibly". Since 2000, the company has had a nutrition policy in place that focuses on healthier products, truth in advertising, and researching the impact of their products. These initiatives were enacted as consumers became more health conscious and concerned about the environmental impact of industries (Emerald Publishing Group, 2013b) Thus, Unilever's campaign to better health and its environmental impact reflected well upon the company. Furthermore, Unilever's focus on global improvement and advertising will be received more widely as the rate of literacy continues to rise worldwide (Unilever Comunications, 2013; UNESCO, 2012). However, natural disasters and consumer preference still impose risks to the corporation.

*Technological Analysis*

Since the 1950's Unilever has internally focused upon research and development. This focus continues today as the company tries to minimize cost through information technology (IT) efficiencies. Specifically, Unilever is using IT to broaden its internet presence and e-business as well as its electronic fulfilment processes. It also is building IT platforms to protect itself against misuse, misuse of information, and disruption of internet business infrastructure (Clark, 2012). While Unilever pursues IT developments to minimize costs, its research and development unit continually works to improve its products and assure a

positive impact. Areas in which increased concentration should be focused include genomics, advanced bioscience, materials science, and nanotechnology (Unilever Communications, 2013).

*Environmental Analysis*

Unilever is currently trying to double its company size while simultaneously decreasing its ecological and environmental impact. The company is specifically targeting "sustainable sourcing, water usage, waste generation and disposal, and greenhouse gas emissions". Yet, there is no guarantee that the company will be able to develop the technologies needed to lower its environmental impact, which could then damage its growth and reputation (Unilever Communications, 2013).

**Porter's Five Forces Analysis**

Porter's Five Forces is an analysis of a business's industry. It focuses on influential economic factors including the threat of new entrants, the threat of substitute products, the bargaining power of customers, the bargaining power of suppliers, and the intensity of competitive rivalry. Three of Porter's five forces refer to competition from external sources while the remainder are internal threats (Porter, 1985).

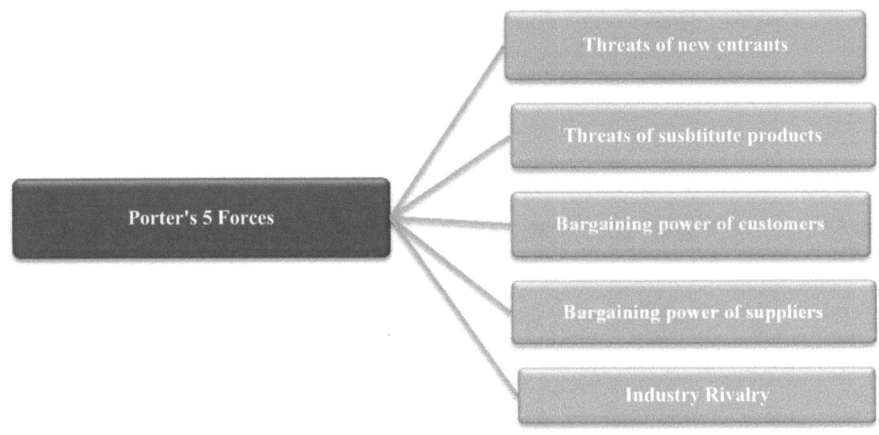

*Threats of new entrants*

The threat of industry consolidation could change the competition in which Unilever competes. If this produces increased competition, price or Unilever stock could plummet. Although Unilever cut two-thirds of its brand portfolio in the 1980s and 1990s, it still controls a large number of brands. This divided attention may also make it susceptible to competitors. Furthermore, Proctor & Gamble, Nestle, and Kraft Foods all have a hold on fast-moving consumer goods. If another company joins the ranks, it could largely impact Unilever's hold on the industry (Unilever, 2013a).

*Threats of substitute products*

While Unilever has spent increasing focus upon its reputation and goal of doing good, this same product may take valuable time and funds from research and development in the consumer and household products. New brands and products have been entering the market threatening consumer loyalty and Unilever's products that are similar. However, Unilever's global presence and size allow it to closely monitor competitors' developments and seize opportunities with its industry. Similarly, it can monitor trends in consumer purchases and product lifecycles to introduce its own new products. Since Unilever has the resources and funds to inquire new, smaller competitors, it also avoids some risk from new competition (Unilever Communications, 2013).

*Bargaining Power of Customers*

Unilever recognizes that maintaining a relationship with consumers is vital to its growth and survival. Consequently, the company has developed capabilities to follow "customer performance and enhance [its] customer relationships". Additionally, consumers are continually looking for new and better products. Therefore, Unilever must continue to focus on research and development to create innovative products and brand communication (Unilever Communications, 2013).

*Bargaining Power of Suppliers*

Unilever has increasingly focused on local buying and manufacturing. This provides an advantage over its suppliers; yet, it also makes them more susceptible to negotiating terms. Unilever has additional strengths in its treatment and agreement with suppliers that helps build loyalty (Unilever Communications, 2013).

*Industry Rivalry*

Proctor & Gamble, Kraft Foods, and Nestle have been long-term rivalries for Unilever. This has allowed Unilever to create policies and practices that allow it to compete. More specifically, the company has a high level of competition with the industry leaders causing a lower level of profit margins. Consequently, Unilever has refreshed its image and relationship with consumers so that they remain loyal and satisfied and focused on research and development in response to competitors (Unilever Communications, 2013). Still, their rivalries have the power to allure customers away from Unilever and towards their attractive substitutes, prices, and marketing techniques (Celen, Erdogan, and Taymaz, 2005).

**Situation (SWOT) Analysis**

SWOT analysis looks at both internal and external influences. Specifically, SWOT analysis's objective is to identify internal strengths and weakness as well as external opportunities and threats. For internal analysis, SWOT uses the strengths of a corporation that may lead to an advantage in the marketplace as well as the weakness that may place it at a disadvantage. For the external analysis, SWOT uses the opportunities in the marco-environment to highlight possible ventures as well as the external threats that may compromise its future (Humphrey, 2005).

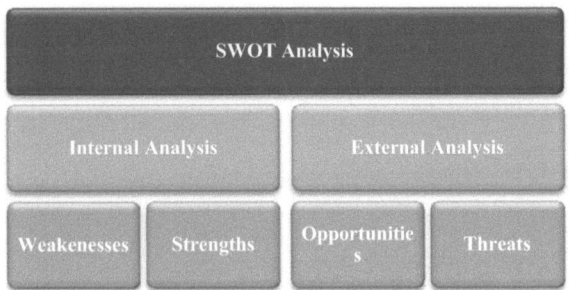

Unilever has strengths in product development, its diverse brand portfolio, strong leadership, motivation of employees, and product diversity. Research and development are a large focus in Unilever's current endeavours (Unilever Communications, 2013). This

supports the aforementioned strengths to continue to build a strong centre in a large, global corporation.

However, Unilever's increased focus on the mission to create a better global future may be an internal weakness as it takes resources, attention, and funds away from company growth. Plus, the size of Unilever results in a complex organizational structure and slower process that must occur over a large scale (Unilever Communications, 2013). These structural, organizational, and mission-based issues compose the company's greatest weaknesses.

Still, opportunities exist for Unilever externally, such as its beneficial reputation to establish a positive position in customers' minds; the rise in purchasing power of developing nations; changing lifestyle and industries; the opening for acquisitions; and consumers' increasing consciousness that aligns with the company's campaigns (Unilever Communications). For example, Unilever's new dedication to the environment has increased customer support and loyalty (Emerald Publishing Group, 2013a). Unilever's current positioning in nation's development and global trends provides the company with vast opportunities to grow.

Still, external threats exist and leave Unilever at risk, particularly in the current global economic climate. Not only does Unilever face strong competitors, it also is susceptible to increasing taxation and financial costs, potential for legal and political strife, information technology risks, and mounting environmental regulations (Unilever Communications, 2013). While global development and economic growth provide opportunities, the result of these same things along with growing concerns about the environment, industry rivalries, and impact of technology threaten the company's success.

Through PESTEL analysis, SWOT analysis, and Porter's Five Forces, we have identified areas in which Unilever should focus attention and make further changes. Since 2009, when Paul Polman became the CEO of Unilever, the fast-moving consumer goods company has worked to transform itself and its public image (Bell, 2013a). These new campaigns have strived to better the global corporation's reputation by increasing sustainability policies and decreasing waste and products detrimental to the environment. Unilever also made company-wide environmental and socio-cultural changes at a vital time when consumers were given increasing choices and became more conscientious. Still, competition and the global economic climate pose threats to Unilever's expansion and business. While the company has situated itself well to have a large, profitable presence in developing countries, taxation and government regulations threaten to hurt profits and

7

corporate expansion. Moreover, Unilever's leadership should keep a continued focus on internal structure and development, specifically IT and product development, so that it can remain a well-functioning consumer goods leader. These conclusions were only derived after completing all three analyses. Each analysis has its strengths; yet, a complete picture of the corporation was only found when putting all three strategic analysis methods together.

# Bibliography

Armstrong, J. Scott. (1986) . "The Value of Formal Planning for Strategic Decisions: A Reply". *Strategic Management Journal*, **7**, 183–185.

Bell, Gareth (2013a) "Doing well by doing good: An Interview with Paul Polman, CEO of Unilever, part 1." *Strategic Directions*, 29 (4) 38-40.

Bell, Gareth (2013b) "Want to change the world? Think differently: An interview with Paul Polman, CEO of Unilever, part 2." *Strategic Directions*, 29 (5) 36-39.

Celen, Erdogan, and Taymaz (2005) "Fasting Moving Consumer Goods: Competitive Conditions and Policies." Economic Research Center Working Papers in Economics

Chung, Ko, Cheung, and Wong (2007) "IT-enhanced order and delivery process of a fast moving consumer goods (FMCG) company." *Benchmarking: an International Journal* 14 (1) 123-139.

Clark, Lindsay. (2012) "Unilever flies the flag for enterprise data warehousing." *Computer Weekly*, 19-21.

Emerald Group Publishing. (2012a) "Unilever's vital shift in direction." *Strategic Direction*, 28 (2), 6-8.

Emerald Group Publishing. (2013b) "In the green corner: how IBM, Unilever, and P&G started winning again." *Strategic Direction*, 29 (5) 19-22.

Helleloid, Duane. (2013) "Unilever: Taking on the World, One Stall at a Time." *Bloomberg Businessweek*, 18-20.

Humphrey, Albert. (2005) "SWOT Analysis for Management Consulting". *SRI Alumni Newsletter.*

Porter, M. (1985) *Competitive Advantage*, New York: Free Press.

Steiner, Rupert. (11/2/2010) "Unilever threatens to pull out of Britain over rising taxes." *Daily Mail.* [Online] Available from: http://www.dailymail.co.uk/news/article-1250083/Unilever-latest-company-threaten-pull-UK-rising-taxes.html [Accessed 17 May 2013].

UNESCO Institute for Statistics. (2012) *Adult and Youth Literacy, 1990-2015: Analysis of data for 41 selected countries.* [Online Report] Available from: http://www.uis.unesco.org/literacy/Documents/UIS-literacy-statistics-1990-2015-en.pdf [Accessed 17 May 2013].

Unilever. (2013a) *Introduction to Unilever.* [Online] Available from: http://www.unilever.com/aboutus/introductiontounilever/ [Accessed 17 May 2013].

Unilever. (2013b) *Our History.* [Online] Available from: http://www.unilever.com/aboutus/ourhistory/ [Accessed 17 May 2013].

Unilever Communications. (2013) *Annual Report and Accounts 2012.* [Online Report] Available from: http://unilever.com/images/ir_Unilever_AR12_tcm13-348376.pdf [Accessed 17 May 2013].

World Economic Forum. (2013) *Insight Report: Global Risks 2013*, 8th Ed.